Zip, or Micrology

Very Short Poems about Very Small Things

Kelly Cherry

Regal House Publishing

Published by Regal House Publishing, LLC
Raleigh 27612

Printed in the United States of America

ISBN -13 (paperback): 978-1-947548-39-8
ISBN -13 (hardcover): 978-1-947548-57-2
ISBN -13 (epub): 978-1-947548-40-4
Library of Congress Control Number: 2018944202

Interior design by Lafayette & Greene
Cover design by Lafayette & Greene
lafayetteandgreene.com
Illustrations © 2018 by C. B. Royal

Regal House Publishing, LLC
https://regalhousepublishing.com

Dedicated to my editor with a thousand thanks

Table of Contents

Intro

You'll find herein
minimal poems
meant to intrigue
and trick you in-
to thinking hard
about small things
from pennies
to strings
and, perhaps,
string theory.

INORGANIC

Power

Children feel powerful when they own a whistle.
Kim Jong-un prefers to launch a missile.

Post-Its

Those little pads of paper in various colors
lighten the heart of any poet about to give a reading.
That barely-there adhesive lets us mark
the places where our poems inhabit the book
we recently published. We love that it doesn't mark up
the book. The glue comes off as easily as it goes on.
We can also write notes to ourselves on our Post-Its,
or number them in the order we'll read the poems.
We stick Post-Its in many places, on computers
as well as margins, on a clock or on one's hand.
When we can't, a Post-It can.

Wayfarer

A button sewn on shirt or dress
is brilliant until it disappears
under unknown duress.

Coaster

A coaster may be sweet or silly.
Either way it keeps the table dry.
Some coasters are rather frilly.
I like a coaster that does not lie.

Parsimony

Snips of thread, if we save them—
maybe from a fraying hem
or heel of an unraveling sock—
may make a skirt or useful smock.

Correction

Consider the hat.
It lingers in the hall
on a hat rack.

Occasionally someone will pick up the wrong hat
and stroll out with it on his or her head.

All one must do is turn around and put it back
and *"All will be well and all will be well and every kind of thing*
    shall be well,"
said Julian of Norwich.

Résumé

A favorite cup proclaims a person's point of view.
A motto may be printed on the cup
or cup otherwise tarted up.
I have a Princeton cup,
a Rockefeller cup,
a cup reminding me that peace is inner,
a cup that says I am the mother of a dog,
and I want to get a Philosophy cup.
That's my résumé in toto.

The Remote

If you have a television,
you have a remote.
It's called a remote because you can turn it on
from a distance, usually the distance between
the television and the sofa.
But when I think of *remote*,
I think of someplace in Italy,
or in Bulgaria.
The South Pole is remote,
the television not so much.

The Right to Choose

I mean to celebrate door knobs.
Because of doorknobs,
we can get where we're going,
a movie, say, or a party,
or a way out.
To grip a door knob is to exercise
your right to enter and leave
and what goes on between here and there
is no one's business but your own.

Symbols

Necklaces are to women
what ties are to men.
They demonstrate a comfortable seriousness,
a certain amount of success,
a kind of class.
Pearls, for example, exude luxury, tidiness, and calm.
A hysterical woman never wears pearls;
she waits until she's un-hysterical.
But diamonds can be crass: don't wear too many.
And though they may not be as dignified as pearls,
necklaces made of glass can be acceptably quirky
and a little to the left.

On Health

Tums will alleviate your heartburn,
aspirin can do almost everything.
We all need a medicine cabinet.
Let's thank it for being dutiful,
Not to mention downright life-saving.

Secretarial

Paperclips and clasps are cousins
as are dribs and drabs,
although the latter are smaller
than clips and clasps.
A clip is a great help
when you want to put pages together
and a clasp binds many more pages.
But sages tell us a drib is less
than a dribble, and a drab—well, a drab
is nothing at all and cannot be found
even at the mall.

Keeping One's Cool

I speak of fans.
Not Beatle fans,
nor movie fans.
Simply fans,
as in fans that churn the air around
when we are so hot we cannot sleep.
When the air is so humid we can hardly breathe.
We turn the fan on, and soon, the sweat
on our faces is wicked off.
Our underarms are no longer disreputable.
A fan is a blessing, and not
such a minor one.

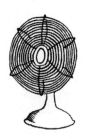

Mica

In New York City, mica made the sidewalks shine.
Shine and glitter, like Broadway shows.
There were stars above
and stars below.
Mica could mesmerize,
or it could mesmerize me.
I didn't have to go to L. A. to see
stars on sidewalks. We had them
right at hand. Or should I say
our feet.

Time

A wristwatch helps us catch the bus
and get to work on time.
Somebody's got to work on time!
Nobody knows enough about it.
Maybe you can begin to understand
the first hour and I'll work on the second.
A third party might give us a helping hand,
and perhaps together we'll discover that
time—yes, time—is the law of the land.

Space

Probably you do not think of the sun and the moon as
    small,
but from where we live, they are relatively small.
The sun's as big as a balloon
(which isn't very big).
The moon's as big as a dime
(which, you must admit, is small)
but stars are barely specks.
So remind yourself that distance plays tricks on us.
The closer you get to the sun and the moon
the more room they take up.
Fortunately, space is colossal.

Modesty

The zipper, zipped, saves your modesty,
nothing falling out of your pants.
Yet sometimes the person in the pants
forgets to zip himself up, leaving on
the outside what should be entirely inside.
In an age of jeans and slacks, the zipper
may also pose a problem for the man's wife.
Hand in hand, they walk beneath the tulip trees,
unaware their zippers are lower than their knees.

Novels

Fine point or bold,
narrow or thick,
the mightier pen
is a Bic.

Tin Cans

They make a mile of noise
rolling down a street
and even more when someone's
Just Married. They help food
last longer than it would
without itself.
A tin can is like an elf:
helpful, but given to
making noise when it oughtn't.

Careless

We found a beautiful glass book case
and paid a thousand dollars.
Then we forgot the name of the store.
They still have our money
and we don't have our bookcase.
Are we reckless?
No, just feckless.
How feckless?
Fucking feckless, that's how feckless.

The Smile

The smile speaks words:
Kindness
Enjoyment
Fondness
Sweetness
Congeniality
Help
A smile is something like a dictionary
but you don't have to look it up.
Just smile.

More Fake News

Let's assume fake news is inorganic,
even though it comes from Donald Trump
who is balefully organic.
Organic as French Fries.
Organic as cheeseburgers.
Organic as fat.
But fake news doesn't cause heartburn
(although it may cause a heart attack)
or indigestion. It may cause the government
to chase rabbits into rabbit holes
and we can only guess at what else they'll find there.

Back Channels

Such channels can go anywhere
 and everywhere.
They are mysterious in their activities.
They wouldn't be in "Organic"
were they not devised by
humans who want to spy
or carry out black ops.
Thus they are both inorganic and
organic. Something like the transgendered
except that the transgendered are brave
and not given to colluding with China and Russia.

Fiscal

Do they still make books with thick pages
of paper pockets for children to save money in?
Nickels and dimes and lots of pennies
taught us to be thrifty and wise
and how to add and subtract.
Then came the day when we took the coins out
to buy ice cream or a toy:
Pure joy.

My Closet

I've purchased hangers with clips attached just so
I can hang up my jeans, which are what I live in
these days, these long unhurried days surrounded
by green trees and birdsong and Beethoven sonatas.
There is now more room in the drawers in the closet.
I am impressed with myself for getting the hangers
because I have very little sense of space.
Clap me on my back, because though I can do
logic, spatial problems are my bête noir.

ORGANIC

High-Spirited

Breezes in trees, like teenagers,
may drape an arm around a date,
hoping for a kiss. But the breeze is
fragrant with tropical fruits and airs
and soon the trees are dancing like rock stars,
shaking their arms and bending and twisting
all in good humor. The sudden wind ceases.

Angels Watching

A nap restores one's energy
unless one's partner snores,
in which case one finds oneself awake
and taking Benadryl
to fall asleep again.
Still,
naps can make us feel
we might be sleeping on a cloud
were the angels not singing so goddamn loud.

Outside from Indoors

Let's applaud windows. They let us see what is
outside, the trees, the bushes, the flowers, the grass
and, of course, the ground, which in the country
is grass but in the city are numerous streets.
We may open the windows to breathe in the smells
of fresh air or close them to say no to the stink
of exhaust. We look out to dream of distance
and the places we'd like to go to, and sometimes
we drift into imagination, as if
the imaginary may be real.
Meantime, the unicorn watches us from the backyard.

A Simple Cold

Your throat is scratchy,
your forehead warm.
Your mother views you
with alarm.
Orange juice and Chicken Noodle,
thermometer and teddy bear are her tools.
Her cool hand on your forehead
makes you feel better right away.
Besides, a sick day
means a day without school.
You are no fool.

New

Newborn babies, even the biggest,
are rather small.
You could probably pack
twenty of them in your closet
with no strain at all.

Their toes are barely there,
while eyebrows are not at all.
But their gurgles establish a sense of self,
reminding us to take them off the shelf.

Surprise

An ordinary day
may be extraordinary
if you want it to be.
Sit under a tree
to hear the squirrels scrabbling up.
Watch the male cardinal
red as daybreak.
We think we are alone and special
but we are surrounded by crowds
of creatures each of which
is a single stitch
in the longest prayer carpet ever woven.

Maturity

Buttercups grew almost everywhere.
Children held them under friends' chins
to see the glow they made.
It was the opposite of shade.

We also made beautiful bracelets
from stems of milkweed.
Beautiful?
Well, we thought it so.

Goldfish

Shy and small, the gold coat of the goldfish shines
like a gold necklace.
No, it's not wearing a necklace.
It is a necklace.

Glory

Never reckless, the goldfinch flies
judiciously, with moderation,
unless something scares it off,
and then it retreats to safer air (not ground),
all its glory soft as down.

Praise for Paper

Where would we be without paper?
No libraries. No universities. No books.
Nothing to write on.
Nothing to make a paper airplane with.
Lists would vanish.
Paper money would be no more
and our pockets would weigh us down
with nickels and dimes and silver dollars.
We have to admit:
paper is significant.

Little Dogs

Little dogs,
not micro,
just little,
bark to defend
like big dogs.
But little dogs
curl up in one's lap
and a big dog
can't do that.
Every dog is a best friend
but a little dog
at day's end
naps in one's lap
like a child
glad to be home
after a day of play.

Hosting a Dinner

Holding books that you have read
and books you have yet to read,
the bookcase is a loyal friend.
It comforts you and keeps you busy,
so much so you find yourself in a tizzy,
having forgotten to prepare dinner
for believers and for sinners,
and they in turn are mad at you
But here's a thought:
A cookbook will get you out of trouble.

Raisins

Raisins are small delights.
A raisin is not a Lincoln or an Audi.
Do people eat them in Saudi
Arabia? I don't know
But I suspect so.

Melania's Coat

That coat cost fifty thousand dollars.
Well, actually a bit more. Made by
Dolce & Gabbana and not even mink,
although that much money suggests minks
or possibly something rarer than mink.
It's silk. She wears the coat with poise and flair,
and perhaps she keeps on staff a personal hair
dresser. Alas, she has to go to bed
with a guy who is fat and mean and crude.
I guess she thinks the money is worth it.
But what does that make her? Or am I a prude?
Maybe so. She certainly dresses well,
and seems more presidential than the president.

Love and Marriage

Lipstick! Now we're talking!
Lipstick is sexy and smart,
and that's only a start.
It's also enticing—and so exciting—to able-bodied men.
A woman may write a message on a mirror
in Orange Delite or Red As Roses.
Her husband will read it, thinking of girlfriends gone,
glad to have his wife's signature on his face.

Rice

It feeds so many.
We should sing its praises.
Right now, in fact.
It keeps the starving from starving.
It's cheap and available.
All kinds of things can be done with it.
My husband serves me fried rice
with celery and zucchini
and something to drink,
wine or water or tea.
It makes me feel globally oriented.
It tastes good.
It's nutritious.
If you want, you can throw it over your head
and your fiancé's head
and bang—you're married! Almost.
You still need a Justice of the Peace.

Shaving

This small poem is for male readers
although my husband demands I include women.
Yes, women can shave their heads, and in America
they shave their legs and underarms.
But men have a closer connection to the act of shaving.
For one thing, they are hairier.
My husband chose to shave his head.
It made his head seem much larger.
He likes it. I like it. Our small dog
likes to lick his large shaven head,
he said. Not the dog. My shaven husband.

Toothbrush

A toothbrush is essential.
We don't want cavities or bad breath.
We want to smile without hiding our teeth.
Our rotting, ancient, godforsaken teeth.
The root canals. The bridges. The lost caps.
The gaps and gullies where once were teeth.
So brush your teeth long and hard
and don't forget to floss
lest love be lost.

Blood Pressure

For some it's too high,
For others, too low.
We medicate accordingly.
On separate occasions
My husband and I have fainted
because our blood pressure was low.
Do we ever meet in the middle?
Sure.
In the middle of the floor.

Compromise

A mouse in a house is a source of dismay.
The humans set out mouse traps with cheese.
The mouse is executed by the trap.
This is joyless for both mouse and human.
Consider throwing out the trap and giving
the mouse the keys. Then he can come and go
quietly as the quietest breeze.

Nature

Billions, trillions of bugs
and they bite, sting, and cling
(e.g., ticks). We live with them
as if they were relatives,
but they are not our aunts
and uncles, not our siblings
or cousins. Let's stomp on them,
swat them, wash them down the sink.
They can try to trick us but they can't think.
They are more like robots than one might think.

Complicated

Door key sounds too much like dorky.
We need another name.
Porky? Corky? Gorky?
Gorky won serious fame,
his literary life entangled
with Soviet paradoxes.
He walked a high wire,
balanced, until he tired and died.

Medical

The Band-Aid on a hurt forefinger
signals the patient's condition:
painful and disabling.
Disabling, because it is not easy
to do anything with your forefinger
when there is a Band-Aid on it.
O the challenges of modern living!
Rip the bandage off.
Pour on the wound a topical antiseptic.
Now you're jiving.

Beauty

The pear tree bears blossoms and the pear blossom
bears impossible beauty, although, of course,
it is not the blossom that bears impossible beauty.
It is we who do, so knocked out by beauty
that we surrender, calling it impossible.
Yet there is the blossom, on the branch, petals
like snow or a snowstorm at the start of sedulous spring.

The Importance of Food

I want to acknowledge the place
of hotdogs under the sun.
With buns they were lunch;
without them, sliced and grilled
in the oven, they were dinner.
Related to them are Vienna sausages.
My father lived on Vienna sausages
and canned sardines. Daily,
a menu of morsels and tidbits.
He'd learned to snack like this
during the Great Depression.
And he was always thin.

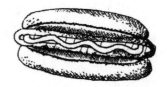

Something *Really* Small

Telomeres:
ends of a eukaryotic chromosome.
Not ends as in objectives.
Ends as in tail ends.
Telomeres protect the ends of our chromosomes
but bit by bit, they get shorter
(not the chromosomes but the telomeres),
which means your life gets shorter.
Your cells cease dividing,
which means no new cells.
That's a bummer.
We get dumber,
and we were pretty dumb
to begin with.

A Wetware Computer

Holy Moley! Someone's invented
a wetware computer.
And what is a wetware computer?
I assume you ask.
A neurocomputer.
A computer that works like a brain.
Not, so far, human brains,
but the brains of leeches have been employed.
Or we could say their neurons have been highjacked.
They can do arithmetic. The brains of leeches.
They are expected soon to be readers of handwritten
   work,
if anyone still writes by hand.
They are being taught to think.
Think, for a moment, about where that takes us.
Maybe to heaven?
Maybe to hell?

Alligator in the Street

At least for a while, and for all I know, now,
alligator high heels were considered smart.
I don't believe the alligator thought that;
I think it did its best not to be caught
by anyone who'd skin it, poor thing.
And were there also alligator briefcases?
I think so. I also think I never want
to meet an alligator in the street.

Cana

When Jesus turned water to wine
an admirer drank himself silly.
"Don't drink and drive," Jesus said,
seeing far, far ahead.
"Oh, I won't," his admirer replied;
"like a horse, I won't be led
to water." "Wine. It is wine
to which you won't be led."
"I won't? So why am I here?"
"As a caution to others," Jesus said
and went to bed.

A New Generation

This time of year, baby birds are being born.
Their parents find good things to feed them:
worms and caterpillars.
The baby birds' beaks open wide.
Down their gullets caterpillars glide.
Later their parents go out to eat
French Fries and dance on the patio,
not doing the Charleston or anything
like that, just swaying back and forth
in each other's feathery wings.

The Merry Brook

The merry brook is having a wonderful time,
skipping and splashing over rocks and against
the banks. The sun reveals glints in the brook,
glints that seem to us promises of
all things good. For a moment, we might begin
to believe there is a God. A God with a cap G.
G for glint, G for God. Alas,
this means nothing, only an alphabetical
accident. Yet it does not dissuade the brook,
the merry brook, from laughing and being merry
(we heard laughter in the bright lilts).

Perspective

On the bedroom floor—a wooden floor—
a scratch that should not be there.
How disrespectful of the scratcher.
The luminous, old-gold wood,
now marred, pains the watcher
unless the watcher can see
that a scratch can be
a thing of beauty.

Our Dog Again

What a delight!
To have room to write
about our tiny dog.
No, he's not teacup
or purse size
but he's so cute
when curled up
we think he's as tiny
as a young pup.

Peace No. 1

Dogs and cats at each other's throat
should be separated by a castle moat.

Peace No. 2

Dog and cat should be separated by a moat
Lest one or the other get its goat.

Peace No. 3

Neither dog nor cat wants to be stuck in a boat
But at least for a little while the dog can float.

Peace No. 4

For each there is a fur coat.
The cat in her coat muses on *Murder, She wrote*.

Peace No. 5

Yet sometimes dog and cat will dote
Upon each other, dog panting, cat très haute.

Advice for Women

When a lover leaves you, do not cry.
Put him out of your mind. A better man
Will show up sooner or later. How will you know?
You know that anyone's better than the former.
Weave flowers in your hair and celebrate.
If he, too, cuts out, do not give up. Always
There is another man somewhere, waiting
For you to find him, and just imagining you
Makes him so hot he can't for the life of him
Cool down.

The Author

Her tears puddled on her manuscript.
She told herself to get a grip.

Then the words came uncannily,
as if they were her long-lost family.

Smart Phones

They are so much smarter than we are.

They know the meanings of words we didn't even know
    were words.

They can locate us, which means we have to hide in a
    closet.

A smart phone's I.Q. is higher than Mozart's I.Q.

My own phone is not smart at all.

In fact, it's dumb.

Not dumb as in mute

but sometimes it's also mute.

A mute phone is not particularly useful.

I'd get a smart phone if I could make it work,

But I can't.

Strings

No, I have decided not
to write about string theory,
because no one knows whether it is valid.
I prefer to write about violins,
whose strings may speak of truth.

Acknowledgments

"The Right to Choose." *The Muse: An International Journal of Poetry.* (India.) Issue 5.1, p. 54.